Pocket ACTIVITY FUN and GAMES

Princess

Sparkly tiaras and beautiful dresses,
fairy-tale creatures and lovely princesses,
all of these things can be found in this book,
so open it up and take a good look!

This PRINCESS book belongs to

....

BARRON'S

What's inside this book?

Puzzles
Connect the dots, find your way through a maze, spot the differences, and more!

Stickers
Track down your stickers and use them on the sticker scenes and anywhere else you want to.

Things to make
Make some note cards on pages 33-36 and fairy cupcakes on pages 40-41. Look out for the pretty paper for decorating things with.

Stories and pictures
There are plenty of things for princesses to write, draw, and paint, so why not start now!

First edition for North America published in 2013 by Barron's Educational Series, Inc.

Text, design, and illustrations copyright © 2012 Carlton Books Limited
An imprint of the Carlton Publishing Group, 20 Mortimer Street, London, W1T 3JW

All inquiries should be addressed to:
Barron's Educational Series, Inc.
250 Wireless Boulevard
Hauppauge, NY 11788
www.barronseduc.com

ISBN: 978-1-4380-0313-9
Library of Congress Control Number: 2012954309

Product conforms to all applicable CPSC and CPSIA 2008 standards.
No lead or phthalate hazard.

Date of Manufacture: February 2013
Manufactured by Leo Marketing, Heshan, China

Printed in China
9 8 7 6 5 4 3 2 1

Author: Andrea Pinnington

You are invited
to join all the
princesses in the
land for a truly
magical adventure.

The magical world of PRINCESSES

SNOW WHITE

A wicked queen tries to kill her beautiful stepdaughter Snow White. who is rescued by prince.

LITTLE MERMAID

This sea princess falls in love with a human.

Complete the princess pictures.

SLEEPING BEAUTY
Sleeping Beauty is cursed by an evil fairy.
She pricks her finger and sleeps for 100 years.

CINDERELLA
Cinderella is treated like a slave by her step family but finds true love with the help of her Fairy Godmother.

How to draw a princess ☆

First, draw a circle for the head, a tiny neck and the top part of the body.

Good start!

Copy each step-by-step drawing into the boxes below.

Then, add puffy sleeves and a big skirt.

Getting there!

3

Now draw some lovely flowing hair, arms and hands, and some teeny, tiny feet.

Almost done!

{4}

Lastly, give her a hat, sparkling eyes, a wand, and a royal bird.

 Great work!

The new story of...

SNOW WHITE

Circle the answers to create your own story.

Once upon a time. there was a wicked ...

STEPMOTHER/ DRAGON/ MATH TEACHER.

The wicked .... was jealous of the lovely ...

SNOW WHITE/ SNOW BLUE/ SNOW DROP.

"Who is the fairest of them all?"

the wicked .... asked her ...

MIRROR/ SERVANT/ TEDDY BEAR.

It replied, "Snow .... ", and so the wicked one set

off to kill her. The wicked .... offered Snow ....

A SHINY RED APPLE/ A ROTTEN BANANA/

A MEATBALL.

Snow .... ate it and ...

FELL DOWN/ SPIT IT OUT/

ASKED FOR MORE

but she didn't die. So the wicked ....

VANISHED MYSTERIOUSLY/

TURNED INTO A LIZARD/

BECAME HER NEW BEST FRIEND

and Snow .... lived happily ever after.

Seeing double

There are 9 differences.
Can you find each one?

Royal pairs

Match up the objects that belong together.

coach

royal letter

sword

brush

comb

pumpkin

king

one shoe

prince

royal envelope

frog

shield

queen

another shoe

Answers are at the back of the book.

Amazing things to do 🌼 with your stickers

1 PLAY with your princess stickers over and over again on the sticker pages in this book.

2 Look out for these other pages where you can use your STICKERS: 16, 26, 27, 30, 31, 38, 39, 51, 60, 61, 76, 77, 78, 79, 80, 81, 84, 85, 91

3 Stick them onto empty JAM JARS. Fill the jars with special things like candy and give them as gifts.

4 Make a SCRAPBOOK about princesses using pictures cut out from magazines. Then use your stickers to decorate the pages.

Super sticker quiz

Which stickers belong in these circles?

Snow White took a bite out of this fruit.

Find an object that turns into a pumpkin at midnight.

It's gold and sparkly and princesses often wear them in their hair.

What does Cinderella leave behind at the ball?

The wicked queen looks into this and asks it questions.

This small vegetable gives a princess a sleepless night.

Answers are at the back of the book.

Help the fairy color in these pretty patterns.

Amazing things to do with your pretty paper

1 Cut out the DRESS SHAPES on the back of the pretty paper. Stick them where they belong (see pages 38-39) and. Presto! Another princess job well done!

2 Use the paper to cover a small notebook to turn it into your own SECRET PRINCESS DIARY.

3 Try designing your own PRETTY PATTERNS that you would like to wear if you were a princess.

Cut out these
DRESS SHAPES.
Find out where they
belong in this book.

Cut out these
DRESS SHAPES.
Find out where they
belong in this book.

Odd ones out?

Circle the objects that don't belong in most normal princess stories.

pea

coach

ring

alien

frog

toaster

mirror

dwarf

bananas

prince

glass slippers

Answers are at the back of the book.

Lots of fun for a princess—fairy magic, stickers, and colored pencils.

Wow—look at the beautiful palace!

Draw some pretty flowers here.

Who is flying on her broomstick?

Which princess pet is playing on the grass?

Draw the princess and her fairy godmother having tea.

Tops
and
bottoms

Fill in the spaces to complete these pictures. Why is the princess so surprised?

How to draw a
Frog prince!

1

Draw a circle for the body.
Then draw two eyes.

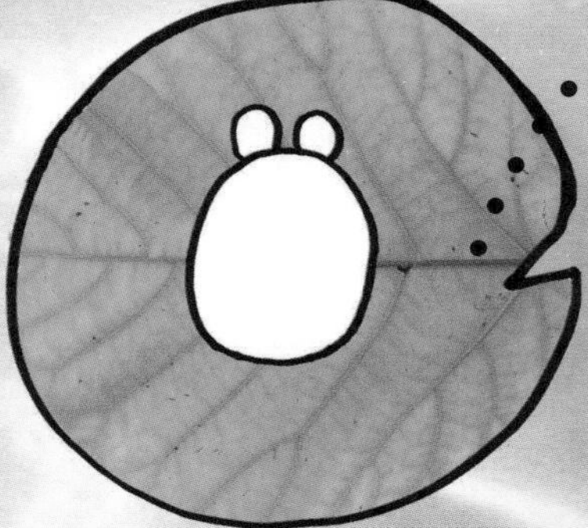

2

Add front legs, back knees.
Add dots to make the frog's
eyes, and a big frog smile.

3

Give the frog prince two
back feet, a tummy and a
crown. Finally, add spots
to decorate.

Draw each step in the lily pads below

Good start!

Getting there!

Great work!

Design your own TIARA

Use your stickers to help you.

Draw the tiara here that you would wear
if you were a princess.

All the parts of a... wicked queen

Complete the picture if you dare!

high eyebrows

very high collar

bright red lips

scary long robes

dark red fingernails

pointy shoes

Royal mail

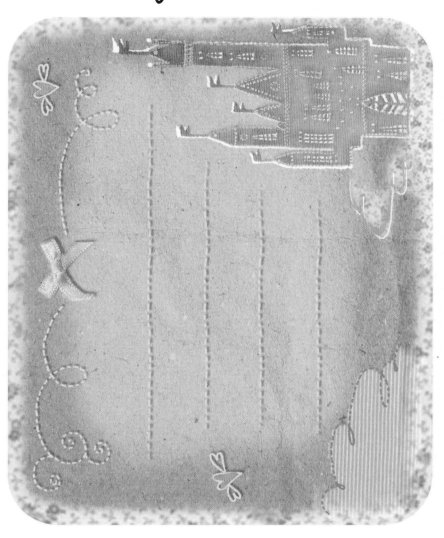

invitation →

To

From

To

From

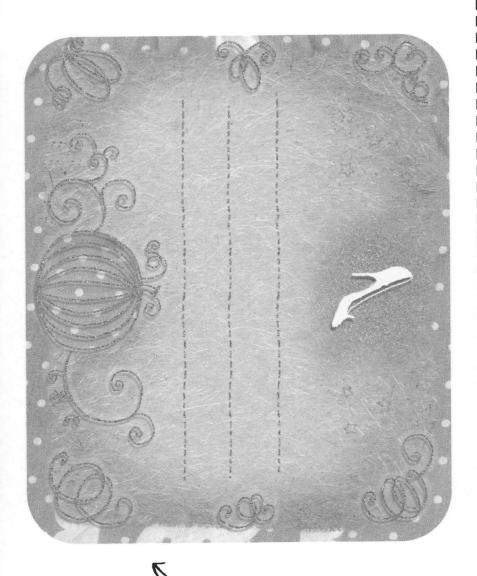

thank you note

The **magical maze**

Help the Prince find the way to Cinderella. Make sure he passes the slipper on his way.

Cinderella

evil stepsister

Start

Prince

evil stepsister

Answer is at the back of the book.

Design-a-dress

Stick your paper dresses onto these pretty princesses. Then, color the hair and tiara of each princess to finish the scene.

Fairy cupcakes

Fairy princesses love to bake.
Now it's your turn.

You will need:

4oz (100g) self raising flour (sifted)

4oz (100g) sugar

4oz (100g) margarine—must be really soft

3/4 tsp baking powder

2 eggs

For the icing:

2oz (50g) butter, softened

3oz (75 g) confectioners' sugar (sifted)

Put all the cake ingredients in a bowl and mix until pale and creamy. Divide the mixture in a cupcake pan and cook for 10-15 minutes in a pre-heated oven at 350°F (180°C). Place on a rack to cool.

To make the icing, mix the butter and confectioners' sugar together until smooth. Spread some icing onto the top of each cupcake and decorate with chocolate chips, cherries, or sprinkles.

When baking, always ask a grown-up for help.

Learning royal moves

at princess school

How to do a ROYAL WAVE

1 Raise right hand in air.

2 Relax hand, then cup it.

3 Twist wrist to left, then right, then left again.

How to CURTSEY

1
Stand with left leg in front of right leg with ankles crossed.

2
Hold skirt out, bend knees. and keep back straight.

3
Slightly bow head, then stand up again and smile.

How to BOW

1
Put right leg forward, right hand on tummy, and left hand by side.

2
Lean forward but keep back straight.

3
Return to upright position.

"Color us in!" say the seven dwarfs

1 purple
2 green
3 yellow
4 red
5 blue
6 brown
7 orange

Match the numbers to the colors.

Princess pet

21

19

23

16

17

20 22 25 26

15

18 ——— 24 27

28

14

29

What type of animal
is this? Connect the
dots to find out.

13

30

12

31

11

32

10

33

9

34

2

3   1

8

35

45 46

4

44

7   5

47

36

6

43

48

42

49

37

41

38

40   39

Answer is at the back of the book.

At the beauty salon

Add hair and makeup to this princess.

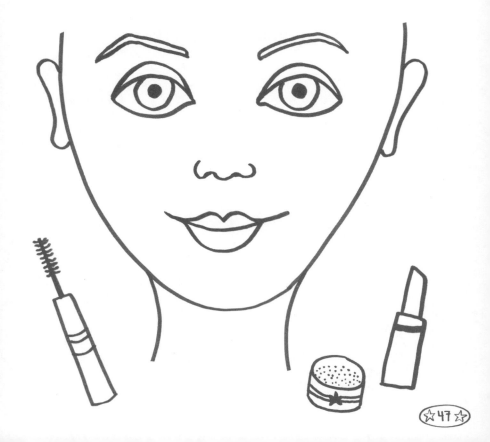

short, curly hair

wild hair

bouncing princesses

Draw their bouncing hair!

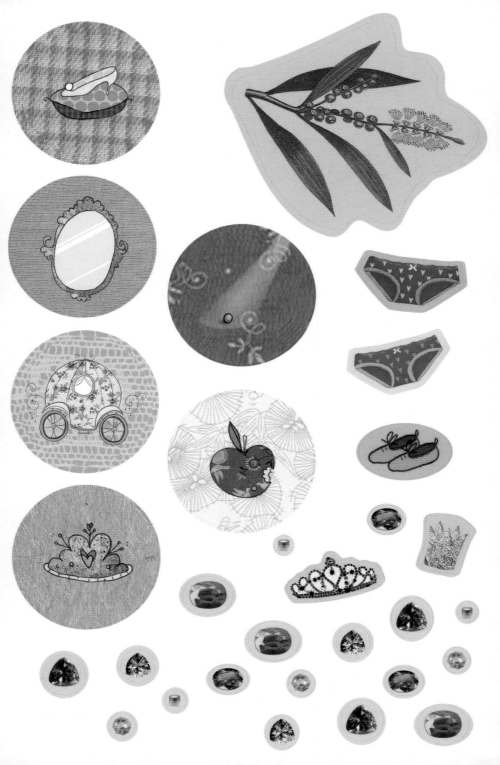

Mila the magical mermaid

Color in this lovely underwater princess and her fishy friends.

Design a cover for this book of...

Fabulous fairy tales

title

title

picture

author

author

The singing princess

Can you spot **12** differences between these princess pictures?

The royal unicorn

Copy the unicorn picture into the
frame above. Try drawing one
square at a time.

Are you a real princess?

How would you TRAVEL to a ball?

skateboard   coach   scooter   rocket

What type of PET would you most like to own?

cat   bat   unicorn   fish

What is your least favorite FOOD?

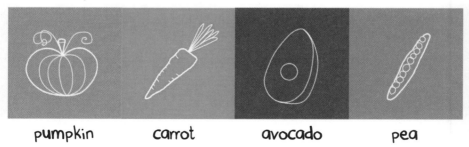

pumpkin   carrot   avocado   pea

Circle your answers.

What are you most FRIGHTENED of?

basketball   spindle   snail   soup

When you look DOWN, what do you see?

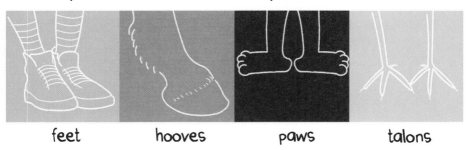

feet   hooves   paws   talons

How many MATTRESSES do you have on your bed?

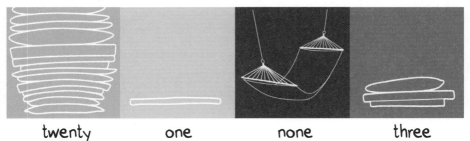

twenty   one   none   three

Answers are at the back of the book.

Draw in **the princess**

and the pea

Find the right home

Follow the lines to see where each princess lives.

Answers are at the back of the book.

Design your own princess palace

ravens

FOR SALE
Big castle with fine views,
25 bedrooms, 4 towers,
and lots of ravens.

castle

tower

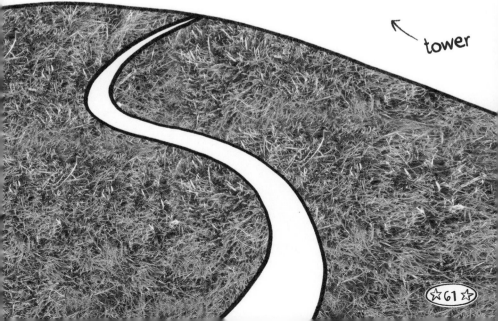

Fairy tale dominoes ☆ ☆ ☆

How to play

1. Put all the DOMINOES you have cut out picture-side down.

2. Take 6 dominoes EACH and leave the rest on the table.

3. The person with the highest DOUBLE domino starts by placing one of their dominoes (picture-side up) on the table.

4. The next player tries to MATCH one side of the domino.

5. If a player cannot go. that player PICKS UP a domino from the pile on the table and misses his or her turn.

Aim of the game

The first person to get rid of all of their dominoes is the WINNER.
If no one can go. then the person with the FEWEST dominoes left wins the game.

Double crown-6
Double castle-5
Double ring-4
Double heart-3
Double apple-2
Double frog-1
Double blank-0

Cut out the dominoes—then find a friend and
get ready to play!

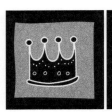 

 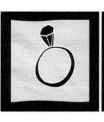 

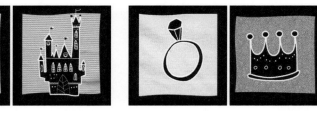 

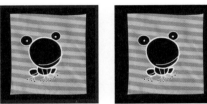

What's inside Prince Charming's head?

Look at these objects for a minute, then turn the page and draw all the things you can remember.

What can you remember?

Draw in the things that were in Prince Charming's head on the previous page. No peeking!

Color in the...

Princess words

TIARA

TRUE LOVE

frog

fairy godmother

dwarf

prince

Can you think of **10** other princess words?

Help the little princess color in these pretty patterns.

What are they saying?

What is the wicked queen shrieking?

What is the princess saying to the frog?

Color in the pictures, too.

Bathtub bubbles

Add some lotions and potions
to the shelves above.

Story checklist

Write or draw all the ingredients you will need for a really good princess story.

☐ For example... a really wicked queen
_____

☐ _____

☐ _____

☐ _____

☐ _____

☐ _____

Now turn the page to write the story.

Write your own princess story

This story is called

Once upon a time

....

....

....

....

....

....

....

....

....

The princess.

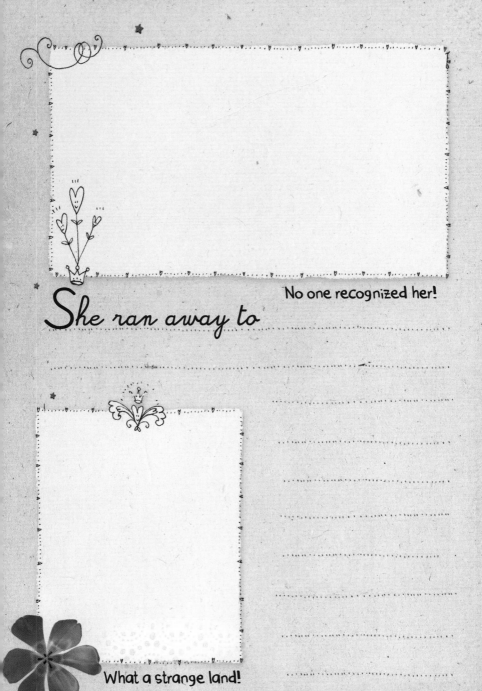

No one recognized her!

*S*he ran away to

What a strange land!

Before long,

A prince appeared on horseback.

At last,

They lived happily ever after.

The End

Royal laundry

Draw in the missing royal clothing.

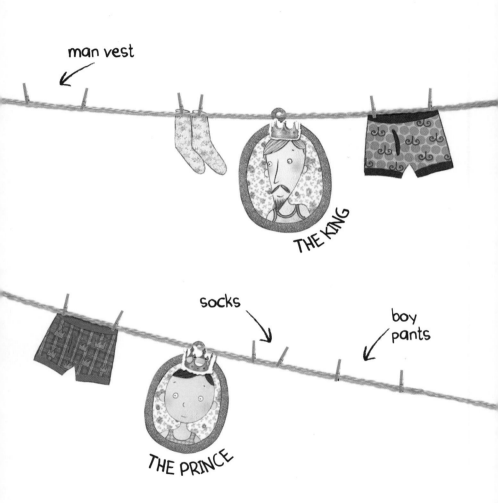

man vest

THE KING

socks

boy pants

THE PRINCE

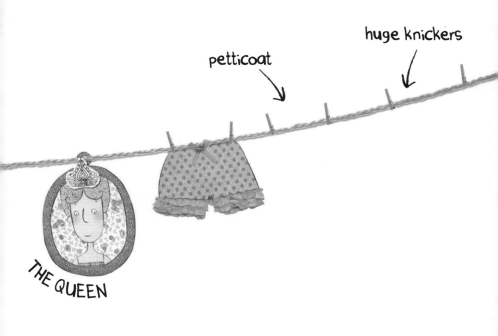

huge knickers

petticoat

THE QUEEN

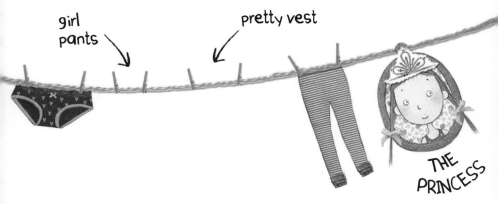

girl
pants

pretty vest

THE
PRINCESS

Princesses don't always smile

happy

sad

annoyed

grumpy

amazed

giggly

How do you think each princess is feeling?
Draw their faces in below.

angry

surprised

cheerful

smiley

scared

thoughtful

At the ball

Use your stickers and colored pencils here.

Snow White's

Long lost photo album

Some of the pictures have faded. Can you fill in the missing pieces?

My stepmother looking into her much-loved mirror

Me outside my home

Holding hands with my pretty
sister, Snow Drop

My favorite pet

Me inside the
glass case

Riding away with my prince

Mirror, mirror on the wall...

Draw a picture of yourself in the mirror.

Crowns and tiaras, slippers and dresses—
fill this space up with clothes for princesses.

What can you see?

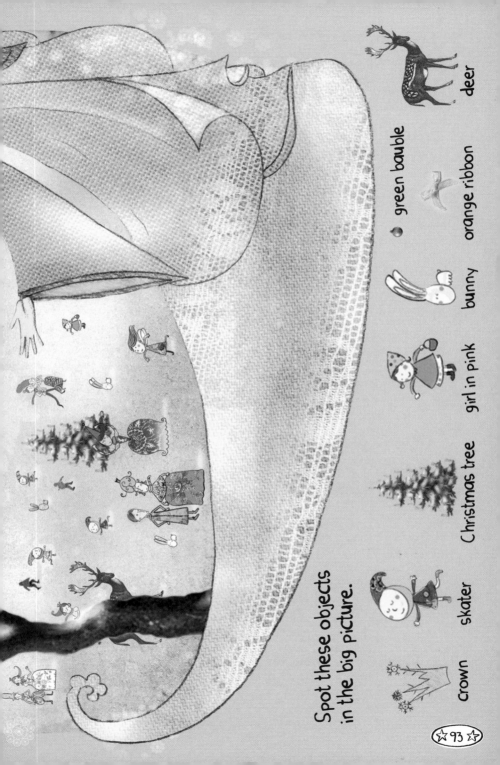

Spot these objects in the big picture.

crown skater Christmas tree girl in pink bunny orange ribbon

green bauble deer

5 really good reasons why I am a

princess

1 I love... _____

2 I like to eat... _____

3 I am nice to... _____

4 I am good at... _____

5 I try to... _____

signed by _____

☆94☆

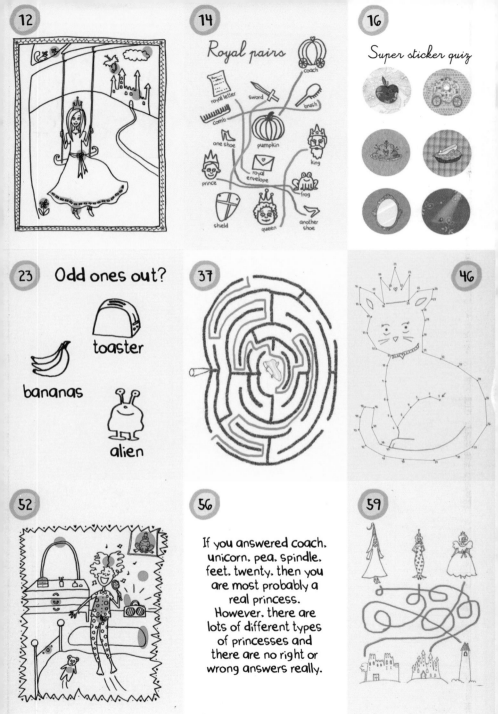

12

14 Royal pairs

coach
royal letter
sword
brush
comb
one shoe
pumpkin
king
prince
royal envelope
frog
shield
queen
another shoe

16 Super sticker quiz

23 Odd ones out?

toaster

bananas

alien

37

46

52

56
If you answered coach, unicorn, pea, spindle, feet, twenty, then you are most probably a real princess. However, there are lots of different types of princesses and there are no right or wrong answers really.

59

ANSWERS

Congratulations

to

....

for being a

REAL PRINCESS

signed by

_____

The Royal Household